JOKE
-O-
RAMA

Silver Dolphin

The croak's on me!

Silver Dolphin Books
An imprint of Printers Row Publishing Group
10350 Barnes Canyon Road, Suite 100, San Diego, CA 92121
www.silverdolphinbooks.com

Printers Row Publishing Group is a division of Readerlink Distribution Services, LLC.
Silver Dolphin Books is a registered trademark of Readerlink Distribution Services, LLC.

All notations of errors or omissions should be addressed to Silver Dolphin Books, Editorial Department, at the above address. All other correspondence (author inquiries, permissions) concerning the content of this book should be addressed to: make believe ideas ltd
The Wilderness, Berkhamsted, Hertfordshire, HP4 2AZ, UK.
501 Nelson Place, P.O. Box 141000, Nashville, TN 37214-1000, USA.

www.makebelieveideas.com

Illustrated by Pedro Demetriou.

ISBN: 978-1-68412-292-9

Manufactured, printed, and assembled in Guangzhou, China, First printing, September 2017. GD/09/17.

21 20 19 18 17   1 2 3 4 5

THERE'S NO LIMIT TO LAUGHTER WITH JOKE-O-RAMA!

Get ready for a book jam-packed with a bonkers banquet of over 250 side-splitting gags and two-line ticklers.

WARNING: Consumption in one sitting could cause aching jaws, permanent smiles, and fractured funny bones!

How do artistic cats decorate their walls?

With paw-traits!

What time is it when an elephant sits on your house?

Time to get a new roof!

Aab! Aab!

Why are tigers striped?

So they won't be spotted!

What kind of animal goes aab, aab?

A sheep walking backward!

Which side of a monkey is the hairiest?

The outside!

How do rabbits go on vacation?

By hare-plane!

What happened when the frog's car broke down?

It got toad!

Why are elephants bad dancers?

Because they have two left feet!

What do you call a bear with no ears?

B!

What do you call cows with a fit of the giggles?

Laughing stock!

What's a sheep's favorite snack?
A baa of chocolate!

Na-na-na-na!

What do you get if you cross
a yellow fruit with an ambulance?
A bana-na-na-na-na-na-na!

What's a cat's
favorite dessert?
Mice cream!

Why don't people like
working in bakeries?
**Because they're
crummy places!**

Which bagel
topping loves riding
roller coasters?
**Scream
cheese!**

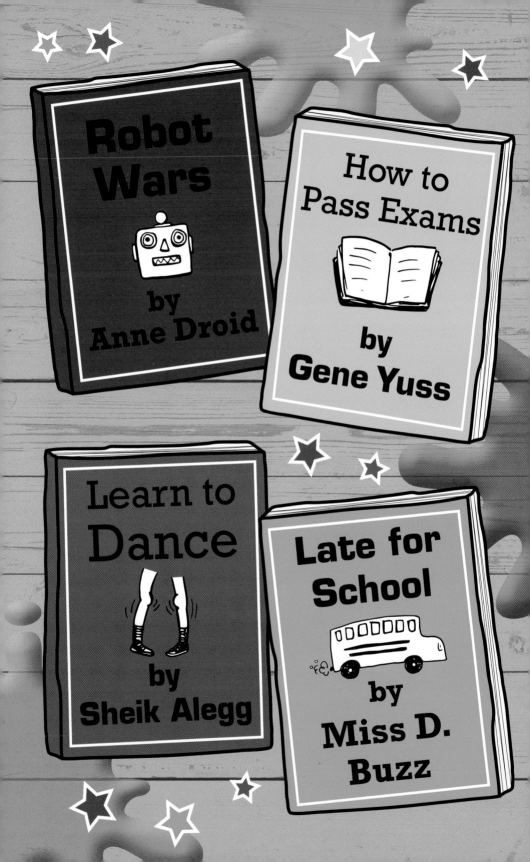

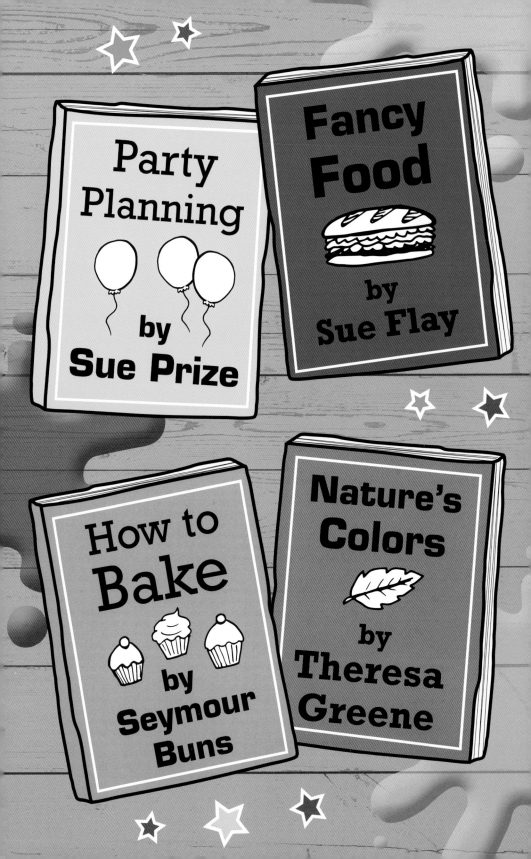

Why do you never meet rich hens?

Because they'll work for chicken feed!

Which *basketball* players can jump higher than the hoop?

All of them—hoops can't jump!

Which pets love bowling?

Alley cats!

Why did the golfer wear two pairs of pants?

In case he got a hole in one!

Which dogs are good at combat sports?

Boxers!

What did the socks say to the hat?

You go on ahead; we'll go on foot!

Which U.S. state has the best-dressed football players?

New Jersey!

What's the hardest thing about skydiving?

The ground!

How do soccer players keep cool in the summer?

They keep close to their fans!

Why was the basketball court so wet?

Because it had been dribbled all over!

What's a cow's favorite city?

Moo York!

Where do cats go to study history?

The mews-eum!

Why is it good to live near horses?

Because they make good neigh-bors!

What did the buffalo dad say to his son when he left for school?

Bi-son!

What do you call a camel with no humps?

Hump-free!

What kind of rabbits own yachts?

Millionhares!

What kind of snake will you find on a building site?

A boa-constructor!

Why didn't the mermaid like the shrimp?

Because it was so shellfish!

When are most chimps born?

Ape-ril!

What do you call a bear caught in the rain?

Drizzly!

Heard any good jokes?

Whenever you hear a good joke,
jot it down here so you won't forget it.

....

....

....

....

....

....

....

....

....

....

....

....

What do you get if you cross a dog with an airplane?

A jet-setter!

Girl to her mom: I've been bicycling to school for three weeks now!

Mom to her daughter: Oh dear, I didn't think it would take that long!

Did you hear about the police investigation into stolen luggage?

It's a very interesting case!

How do snake charmers keep their windshields clean?

With windshield vipers!

Why did the farmer's boat sink?

Because it was filled with leeks!

What's big and scary and has one wheel?

A monster on a unicycle!

What's the laziest machine on a building site?

The bull-dozer!

Which type of market should you never take a dog to?

A flea market!

Which ships have lots of students on board?

Scholarships!

What do you get when dinosaurs crash into cars?

Tyrannosaurus wrecks!

Why did the snowman go to the vegetable shop?

He wanted to pick his nose!

What type of music do elves listen to at the North Pole?

Wrap music!

Which school supplies should always be obeyed?

Rulers!

Why are protractors smart?

Because they have 180 degrees.

How do bees get to school?

They take the school buzz!

What's a runner's favorite school subject?

Jog-raphy!

Why is Florida full of locks?

Because of all the Keys!

Which islands do sheep like best?

The Baa-hamas!

Why didn't the skeleton want to go skydiving?

Because he didn't have the guts!

Why do fish get good grades?

Because they stay in schools!

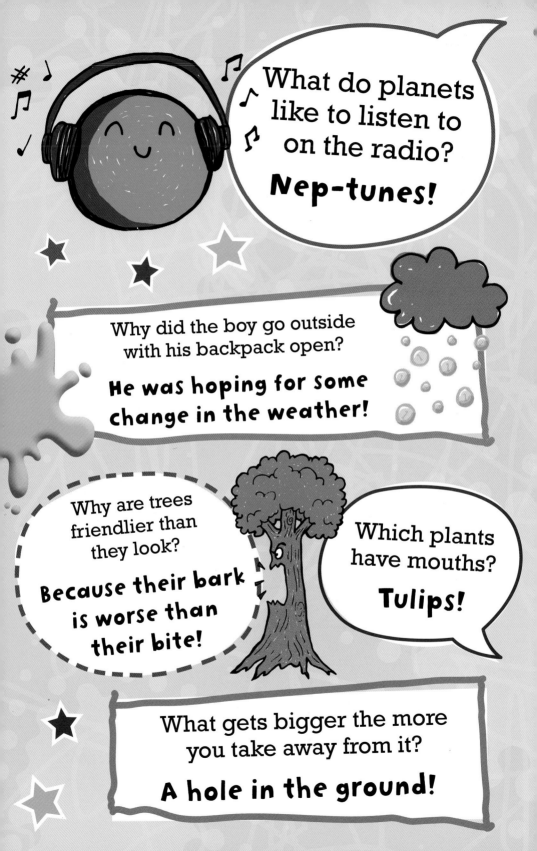

Why do grapes have big families?

Because they love raisin kids!

Why was the strawberry late for work?

It was stuck in a jam!

When do astronauts have their sandwiches?

At launch time!

Which *books* are like *fruitcakes*?

History books, because they're full of dates!

What did the milk say when the cream turned sour?

Yogurt to be kidding!

Why did the donut visit the dentist?

It needed a filling!

Why did the boy put his cake in the freezer?

Because he was trying to ice it!

What did the doctor say to the man with carrots in his ears?

You're not eating properly!

What's brown and hairy and sits by the pool?

A coconut on vacation!

What do you call an apple in a bad mood?

A crabapple!

Hmmm, hmmm, hmmm!

Why was the car engine humming?

Because it didn't know the words!

When can a tortoise go as fast as a bus?

When it's sitting on a bus seat!

Do trains have eyes?

No, but they do have engine-ears!

Why was the train never behind schedule?

Because it was always on track!

Why did the dinosaur go to the garage?

His car had a flat tire-annosaurus!

Why did the spider buy a laptop?
To build a website!

How do you stop your laptop's battery from running out?
Tie its laces together!

Why was the computer late for work?
It had a hard drive!

Why did the computer go to the restaurant?
It wanted a byte to eat!

Why do keyboards take so long to put on their shirts?
Because they have so many buttons!

What do monsters put on their laptops? **Scream savers!**

Where did the computer geek kick her ball? **Internet!**

Why did the man put bumpers on his computer? **He was afraid it might crash!**

Why shouldn't you leave cheese on your computer? **Because the mouse might eat it!**

Which search engine do slime monsters use? **Gooo-gle!**

Where do frogs like to picnic? **Under croak trees!**

Which chickens tell the best jokes? **Comedi-hens!**

Why did the rabbit move into a condo? **She was bored with the hole thing!**

How long should a giraffe's legs be? **Long enough to reach the ground!**

What type of dog did the magician buy? **A labra-cadabra!**

Which circus performers have wings?

Acro-bats!

What kind of movies do rabbits like?

Ones with hoppy endings!

How do snails settle arguments?

They slug it out!

Why do cats keep away from trees?

Because they're afraid of their bark!

What did the cat say when it bumped its head?

Me-OW!

When are hamburger chefs busiest?
On fry-day!

Why did the Italian chef throw away his spaghetti?
Because it was pasta its expiration date!

Why did the barber quit his job?
He couldn't cut it!

Why did the waitress quit her job in space?
Because the restaurant had no atmosphere!

Which Star Wars character loves fishing?
Darth Wader!

What do you say to a thirsty dinosaur? **Tea, Rex?**

Why did the maze designer quit his job? **He kept getting lost in his work!**

What did the baker give his wife on Valentine's Day? **Flours!**

What did the detective say to his new boss? **Policed to meet you!**

Why did the mattress become a spy? **It wanted to be undercover!**

Heard any more good jokes?

Write them here!

....

....

....

....

....

....

....

....

....

....

....

....

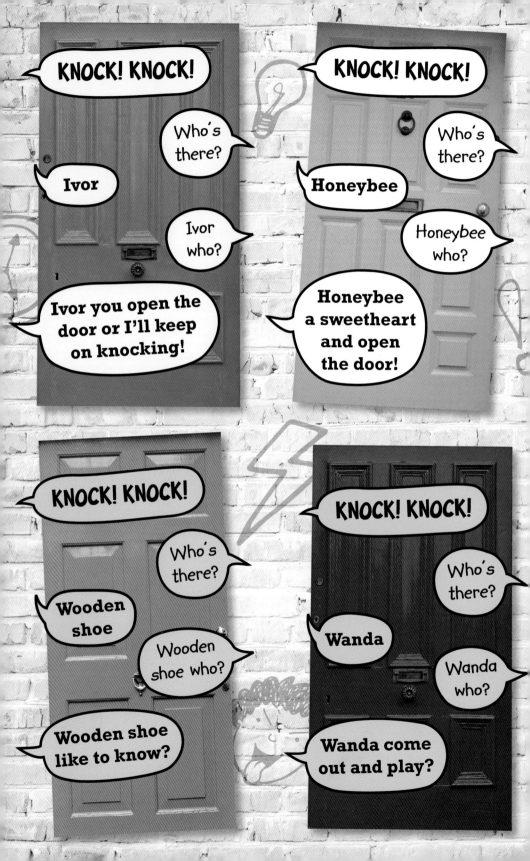

Which sport is often found in backyards?

Fencing!

Where do badminton players go to become famous?

Volleywood!

VOLLEYWOOD

Which insects can't catch?

Fumble bees!

Why don't fish play tennis?

Because they don't want to be caught in the net!

Which sport do birds play in winter?

Ice hawkey!

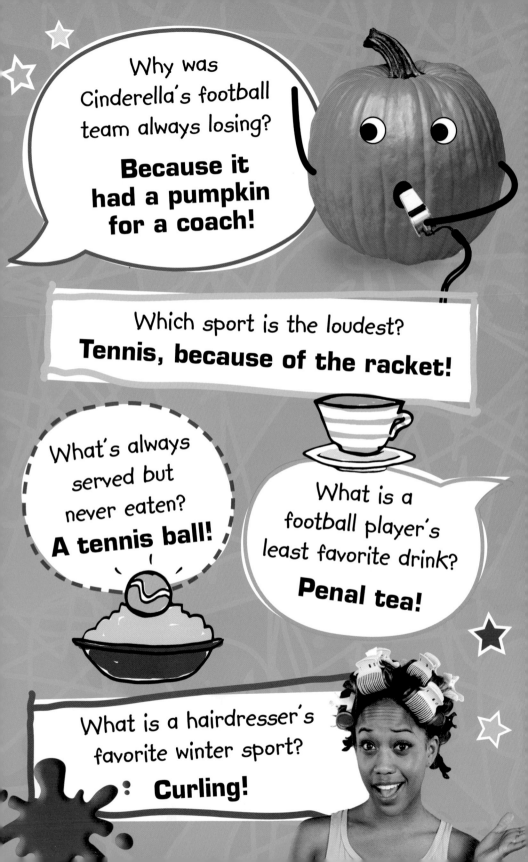

What's the easiest way to get straight A's?
Use a ruler!

Did you hear the one about the girl who left her pencil sharpener at home?
She couldn't see the point!

What's the first lesson at gardening school?
Weeding and writing!

Why was the math exam worrying?
Because it had so many problems!

Why did the student walk to school on stilts?
Because she wanted a higher education!

Where do pirates go on vacation?

Arrr-gentina!

What's the best way to get to school?

On the sylla-bus!

Why did the music teacher bring a ladder to class?

So her students could reach the high notes!

What do you learn first at baseball school?

The alpha-bat!

Why do libraries need elevators?

Because they have so many stories!

What do trees wear to the beach?

Swimming trunks!

What's an octopus's favorite playground ride?

The sea saw!

How do you know if a farmer is good at his job?

He'll be out standing in his field!

How can you tell if the ocean's in a good mood?

It waves!

What happens if you slip on a mountain?

You hit rock bottom!

What did the bee say to the sunflower?

Hi, Honey!

What do you give a lemon tree with a broken branch?

Lemon aid!

What did the beaver say to the log?

It's good to get to gnaw you!

Which is the saddest tree in the forest?

The weeping willow!

What's smartly dressed and growls on your lawn?

A dandy lion!

What do you call a monster wearing earphones?

Anything—he can't hear you!

Where do European hamsters live?

Hamsterdam!

What do you call a cow on a roller coaster?

A milk shake!

Why are bulls louder than cars?

Because they have two horns!

How are crimes solved in swamps?

By investi-gators!

Where do sheep go for haircuts?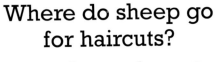

The baa-bers!

Which dogs always know the time?

Watch dogs!

Why do dragons rest during the day?

So they are ready to fight knights!

How do you find a pesky mosquito?

Start from scratch!

What's a cat's favorite type of show?

A mew-sical!

What's the best way to prepare dinner in space?

Planet!

What do you get if you cross a dog with a *sausage*?

Pupperoni!

Why did the mouse take a bath?

So it would be squeaky clean!

What's the best day to eat ice cream?

Sundae!

Which cracker topping is always sad?

Blue cheese!

Why did the man put two bananas on his feet?

Because he wanted a pair of slippers!

Why do bananas stay out of the sun?

Because they peel easily!

Why did the orange go to the gas station?

Because it ran out of juice!

Why did the Italian meal go to Vegas?

For a pizza the action!

Which fruit can fix your shower?

Plum-ers!

Did you hear about the woman who walked on her laptop?

She got webbed feet!

Why was the computer geek's house cold?

Because he never closed Windows!

Did you hear about the boy who was on his computer all night?

He'd have been a lot more comfortable in bed!

Why is shopping on the Internet dangerous?

Because your cart might fall off the computer!

How did the computers afford to buy a gift?

They all chipped in!

What did the boy do when his screen froze?

He put it in the microwave!

How do lumberjacks start their computers?

They log in!

Why did the cat get bored with computing?

Because it couldn't scare the mouse!

How do hungry computers eat their lunch?

With mega bites!

Why are flies scared of computers?

They don't want to get caught in the web!

Why didn't the boy take the bus to school? **It was too big to fit through the door!**

How do pilots like their bagels? **Plane!**

Why couldn't the duck see where he was going? **Because his windshield was quacked!**

Why do train guards look so tall? **Because they wear platform shoes!**

Why was the train found guilty? **Because it had a clear loco-motive!**

Why was the railway driver
bad at his job?

Because he wasn't trained!

What do you call a jumbo jet
going the wrong way?

An error-plane!

Why would
Peter Pan make
a bad pilot?

**Because he would
Neverland!**

Why are tires
so expensive?

**Because of
inflation!**

Why was the
gas angry with
the truck?

**Because it took
him for a fuel!**

Why did the lumberjack fail his exams?

Because he was stumped!

Why did the teacher find it hard to concentrate?

Because she couldn't control her pupils!

What do you call a boy with an encyclopedia in his back pocket?

Smarty pants!

What stays in one place but travels all over the world?

A postage stamp!

Which month is the shortest?

May, because it's only got three letters!

Heard some more good jokes?

Don't forget them! Write them here.

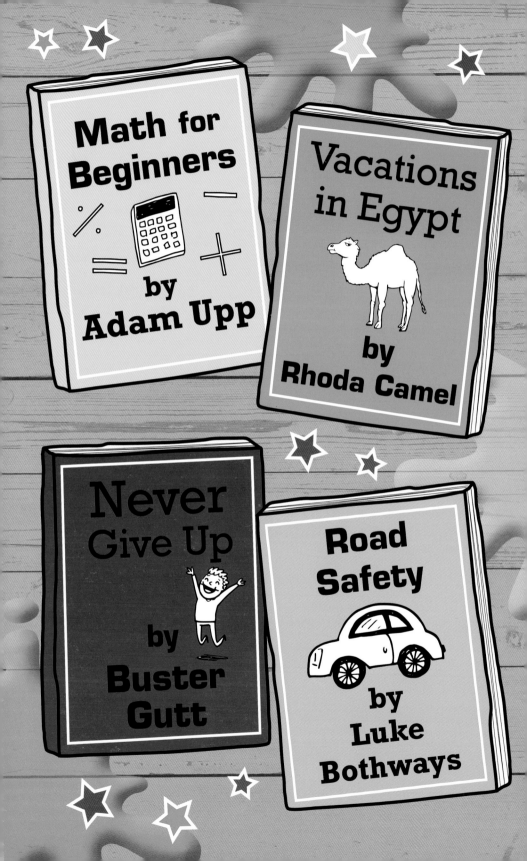